Thanksgiving
A Way of Lifestyle

Benjamin Ayim Asare

BOOKS BY DR. BENJAMIN AYIM ASARE

English Books

1. From Deliverance to Inheritance

2. Life is a Priceless Treasure

3. The Hand of the Diligent Will Rule

4. The Anointing is in the Assignment

5. Discover your Ministry in the Local Church

6. Thanksgiving, A Way of Lifestyle

Italian Books

7. La Vita è un Tesoro Inestimabiled

8. Dalla Liberazione all'Eredità

AVAILABLE FROM BENCOM PUBLICATIONS, AMAZON.COM AND OTHER RETAIL OUTLETS

Thanksgiving
A Way of Lifestyle

Benjamin Ayim Asare

BOOK TITLE: *Thanksgiving, A Way of Lifestyle*

WRITTEN BY Dr. BENJAMIN AYIM ASARE
ISBN: 978-0-9575775-2-7
eBook ISBN: 978-0-9575775-3-4

Copyright 2017 Benjamin Ayim Asare

All rights reserved. No part of this publication may be reproduced or transmitted in any form or by any means, electronic or mechanical including photocopying, recording or any information storage or retrieval system, without prior permission in writing from the publishers.

First published in Italy in 2017 by **BENCOM**
Via Ghiberti, 1
28100 Novara
Italy

Email: bayimasare@yahoo.it
Email: focicatmissions@yahoo.com
www.benjaminayimasareministries.com

Unless otherwise indicated, scripture quotations are taken from the New King James Version®. Copyright © 1982 by Thomas Nelson, Inc. Used by permission. All rights reserved.

*Where scriptures appear with special emphasis (**in bold**, italic or <u>underlined</u>) we have edited them ourselves in order to bring focused attention within the context of this subject being taught.*

Table of Contents

	Introduction	7
Chapter 1	Be Thankful in All Things	9
Chapter 2	The Essence of Thanksgiving	15
Chapter 3	Celebrating the Annual Thanksgiving and Harvest	31
Chapter 4	Dealing With Ingratitude	55
Chapter 5	His Love and Promises are Forever	67

Introduction

Thanksgiving is the expression of appreciation and gratitude to someone who has given you a gift or help of any kind. We may all have other individuals who have blessed or touched our lives in some way and we need to thank them for their kindness and generosity.

Whatever blessing or gift we receive from parents, friends and loved ones are goodness from the Lord. He is the one who touches people's hearts to do well. You must understand that every perfect gift comes from the Father of light, God Himself.

What does God think of thanksgiving? He is blessed and honoured by it because a life of thanksgiving is the mark of a Christian who knows God's character and His position as

God alone. The Lord is the giver of all good gifts and He is worthy of thanksgiving. Since God's qualities are not hidden, thanksgiving is not optional.

All mankind owes God a great debt of gratitude. More than two thousand years ago God gave an indescribable gift, His Son, Jesus Christ. "Thanks be to God for his indescribable gift" (2 Corinthians 9:15 NASB).

This gift of God is the essence of all giving. When we were all dead in trespassing He gave us life through His Son, Jesus Christ. And apart from this wonderful gift of salvation, many gifts that could not be mentioned have been entrusted into our hands. It is the duty of all nations, people and individuals to acknowledge the providence of Almighty God, to obey His will, to be grateful for His benefits, and humbly implore His protection and favour. Within this book you will discover the importance of thanksgiving and every bumper crop you have attained in life.

You will also discover how to appreciate people whom God uses to bless your life. Everything we enjoy in the present and coming age is a gift from God, worthy of thanksgiving. All people including non Christians and Christians enjoy the blessings of the Lord.

CHAPTER 1

Be Thankful in All Things

I was much optimistic when I was preparing a message for our church's annual Harvest and Thanksgiving service November, 2014. As I was pondering on the subject my mind reflected back to my childhood days, when my mother used to give me gifts, in those years I smiled and with an enthusiastic face received the presentation and with an attempt to celebrate the gift, she would ask me, "And what do say?" Then would I respond with a joyful tone, "Thank you mama." At that tender age my mother was teaching me how to express thanks to people.

Thankfulness or appreciation is a feeling or attitude in acknowledgment of a benefit that one has received or will receive.

THANKSGIVING – *"todah"* (thanks-giving) – means raise adoration and is taken from the verb *"yadah"* to give thanks, to praise, to lift or extend one's hands in thanks to God with something.

> *O Come, let us sing for joy to the LORD; Let us shout joyfully to the rock of our salvation. Let us come before His presence with thanksgiving; Let us shout joyfully to Him with psalms. For the LORD is a great God, And a great King above all gods, In whose hand are the depths of the earth; The peaks of the mountains are His also. The sea is His, for it was He who made it; And His hands formed the dry land. Come, let us worship and bow down; Let us kneel before the LORD our Maker.*
>
> *(Psalms 95:1-7 NASB)*

The actual first official ceremony of Thanksgiving in the bible is listed in (Leviticus 7:11-15). God ordained a practice of specific instructions to show gratitude. Gratitude is the door that opens peace in our hearts. God's design for mankind is that giving thanks means receiving peace.

> *Be careful for nothing; but in everything by prayer and supplication with thanksgiving, let our request be made known to God. And the peace of God, which passes all understanding, shall keep your hearts and minds in Christ Jesus.*
>
> *(Philippians 4:6-7 KJV)*

> *For since the creation of the world God's invisible qualities – his eternal power and divine nature - have been clearly seen, being understood from what has been made, so that people are without excuse. For although they knew God, they neither glorified him as God nor gave thanks to him,*

> *but their foolish hearts were darkened. Although they claimed to be wise, they became fools.*
> *(Romans 1:20-22 NIV)*

The absence of glory, honour and thanksgiving ascribed to God, leads to darkened hearts and futile thinking. No human being can give an excuse for not recognizing who God is. The creations of the world we live in, the handiwork of the Lord God Almighty are enough for every human to know Him as a supreme sovereign God. May God's people receive wisdom as we glorify His eternal power and divine nature with praise and thanksgiving! The Lord is the giver of all good gifts and He is worthy of thanksgiving.

Since God's qualities are not hidden, thanksgiving is not optional. Thanksgiving is mandatory. You did not have anything that you did not receive. No one has ever been to a higher life pursuit on his own human effort. Somebody helped you before you reached where you are now and it's the Lord's doing.

> *Whatever is good and perfect comes to us from God above, who created all heaven's lights. Unlike them, he never changes or casts shifting shadows. In his goodness he chose to make us his own children by giving us his true word. And we, out of all creation, became his choice possession.*
> *(James 1:17-18 NLT)*

Everything we enjoy in the present and coming age is a gift from God worthy of thanksgiving. All people including non Christians and Christians enjoy the blessings of the Lord. God does not change His mind towards mankind, when we talk of rain, sun, air, moon and the shining stars etc. God is at work for our good and His glory.

Biblical thanksgiving does not focus on our circumstances, but on the character of God. Circumstances change; God does not. God's love and promises are forever. Since circumstances and situations do not change God, it means His faithfulness and righteousness are forever. He is the only supreme and sovereign God who needs our thanks without discrimination.

Being Thankful to God

In Christianity, gratitude is an essential part of the act of worship and a part of every aspect of a worshiper's life. According to the Word of God, all things come from God and because of this, gratitude is extremely important to the followers of Christ. The scriptures are filled with the idea of gratitude. Two examples included in the Psalms are "O Lord my God, I will give thanks to you forever," and "I will give thanks to the Lord with my whole heart" (Psalms 30:12; Psalms 9:1).

The Christian prayers also often incorporate gratitude beginning with the "Shemmah," (my Lord is Present) where the worshiper states that out of gratitude, "You shall love the Eternal, your God, with all your heart, with all your soul, and with all your might" (Deuteronomy 6:5 NASB).

Give thanks in all circumstances, for this is God's will for you in Christ Jesus. In giving thanks to God; don't forget from where your blessings come. "Praise the Lord, O my soul, and forget not all His benefits" (Psalms 103:2 NIV).

Give thanks for you are redeemed! "Oh, give thanks to the LORD, for He is good! For His mercy endures forever. Let the redeemed of the LORD say so, whom He has redeemed from the hand of the enemy" (Psalms 107:1-2).

Give thanks for all the good God does for you. "Oh, that *men* would give thanks to the Lord for His goodness, and for His wonderful works to the children of men!" (Psalms 107:8) We can be thankful for how God has rescued us from our enemies. "He delivers me from my enemies. You also lift me up above those who rise against me; You have delivered me from the violent man" (2 Samuel 22:49).

Thanksgiving should be an attitude of your life. Even in the mix of challenges, you are to thank the Lord. That is what the bible says. Let us have the attitude of Daniel even in the lion's den, he praised and thanked the Lord knowing that He can deliver him. Daniel gave thanks even in the face of the lion's den – it was his habit.

"Now when Daniel knew that the writing was signed, he went home. And in his upper room, with his windows open toward Jerusalem, he knelt down on his knees three times that day, and prayed and gave thanks before his God, as was his custom since early days" (Daniel 6:10). **Thanksgiving was part and parcel of Daniel's life, it was his lifestyle.**

Giving of thanks should become a custom and integral part of every person's life. Each and very person living on planet earth receives help or blessing daily, you need to recognize and identify the specific blessings, count them and name them one by one and see what the Lord is doing in your life.

Chapter 2

The Essence of Thanksgiving

The main reason why you must thank God is that there is nothing you have that you did not receive. That means you have nothing to show up on your own. All things, I mean all things were given to you by the Lord. Until people come to this point of revelation, thanksgiving would be optional. But thanksgiving shouldn't be an option; it must be a way of life.

> *I will bless the Lord at all times; His praises shall continually be in my mouth.*
>
> *(Psalms 34:1)*

> *Give thanks always for all things to God the Father in the name of our Lord Jesus Christ.*
>
> *(Ephesians 5:20)*

THANKSGIVING, A WAY OF LIFESTYLE

In every thing give thanks; for this is the will of God in Christ Jesus for you.
(1 Thessalonians 5:18)

As a believer, thanksgiving must be a lifestyle. Circumstances may deceive us but God's Word tells us: "We know that in all things God works for the good of those who love him, who have been called according to his purpose" (Romans 8:28 NIV).

King David had a lifestyle of thanksgiving. He said, "I will bless the Lord at all times," during bad times and good. Because all things work together for the good of those who love God. In Psalms 73, Asaph was perplexed at the prosperity of the wicked while the godly faced difficulties and trials. However, he reminded himself that God alone was his provision, counsel, strength, desire and portion. He knew from God's Word the fate of those who are far from God and he remembered that it was good and right for him to be near God, yet he refused to offer thanksgiving for that all God had done.

Those who have the salvation of God through faith in Jesus Christ know that the secret to peace is found in thanksgiving. The apostle Paul, writing to the Philippians, said, "Do not be anxious about anything, but in everything by prayer and petition, with thanksgiving, present your requests to God. And the peace of God, which transcends all understanding, will guard your hearts and your minds in Christ Jesus" (Philippians 4:6-7 NIV). By submitting our requests to God with a thankful heart, we receive peace that transcends all understanding.

Thanksgiving is integral to a right relationship with God. It is the hallmark of a true follower of Jesus Christ because thanksgiving honours God, bringing glory to His name and blessings beyond measure.

God's Word teaches that thankfulness ought to be a way of life. But in the reality of our daily lives, it is so easy for discontentment, murmuring, complaining, criticizing, or even bitterness to displace the "attitude of gratitude."

Cultivating a thankful heart will result in speaking thankful words. But we all need periodic reminders to be thankful, and, for most of us, developing the habit of thankfulness may require some practice. Paul instructed the Ephesian believers to "give thanks always for all things..." (Ephesians 5:20) All things means all things – bad times and good.

Recognize and Identify the Specific Blessings

You need to cultivate a habit of thanks in even smaller things. If you will notice and appreciate the little, little things that people render to you, you may develop a lifestyle of gratitude. Someone has defined gratitude as, "learning to recognize and express appreciation for the benefits which a person received from God and others."

Before you can express gratitude, you must take time to recognize and identify the specific blessings that you have received from God and others. Make a list of all the material and spiritual blessings you can think of that you have received from the Lord. Then stop and thank God for each item on your list.

In the book Colossians 1:12-14, Paul teaches many reasons for giving thanks to God.

1. He qualified us to share in the inheritance of the saints in light
2. He delivered us from the domain of darkness
3. He transferred us into the kingdom of His Son
4. He redeemed us, providing the forgiveness of sins

The Lord has Qualified us to Share Inheritance

First and foremost, before a person qualified to obtain something that means he has provided or has the abilities to perform a particular task. For an example, if you want to apply for a particular job or carrier you have to prove your qualification or credential that qualifies you for that job. If you failed to prove the requested qualifications you will be disqualified.

In our case as Gentiles we were living in this world having no hope and without God, but now in Christ Jesus we have been qualified as the sons of God by the blood of Christ. We called ourselves Christians because we now inherit everything that belongs to Christ Jesus. We are now heirs together with Him. To qualify simply means to make sufficient and, secondarily, to entitle, just as the Lord honoured the children of Israel by giving that land of Canaan as an earthly inheritance, so He has honoured every Christian with the potential of obtaining the inheritance of spiritual Canaan.

Inheritance is a property, a right or title that fathers or parents give to their children. To inherit is to succeed as heir. Through Christ Jesus, we the sons of God are legally transmitted to an heir, all things that God has automatically given to us. We have a heritage in Christ Jesus.

In him we have obtained an inheritance, having been predestined according to the purpose of him who works all things according to the counsel of his will, so that we who were the first to hope in Christ might be to the praise of his glory. In him you also, when you heard the word of truth, the gospel of your salvation, and believed in him, were sealed with the promised Holy Spirit, who is the guarantee of our inheritance until we acquire possession of it, to the praise of his glory.
(Ephesians 1:11-14 ESV)

You were qualified simply because when you heard the gospel of Christ you believed and accepted Him as your Lord and Saviour. And from that time the Holy Spirit sealed you and guaranteed your inheritance.

We were dead in this life until through His mercy, He causes us to be alive again to a living hope through the resurrection of our Saviour Jesus Christ. We have a heavenly inheritance that can never be destroyed. This property has been kept for us as Christians.

Blessed be the God and Father of our Lord Jesus Christ! According to his great mercy, he has caused us to be born again to a living hope through the resurrection of Jesus Christ from the dead, to an inheritance that is

imperishable, undefiled, and unfading, kept in heaven for you, who by God's power are being guarded through faith for a salvation ready to be revealed in the last time.
(1 Peter 1:3-5 ESV)

Delivered us from the Domain of Darkness

Christ has delivered us from spiritual death, sickness and hostile situations in general. This rescue is including both present deliverance and future. He has conveyed us. Conveyed refers to the deportation or transference of captured armies or populations from one country to another. The Lord has delivered us from this world to His eternal kingdom.

Giving thanks unto the Father, who has made us fit to be partakers of the inheritance of the saints in light. For he has delivered us from the power of darkness, and has translated us into the kingdom of his dear Son.
(Colossians 1:12, 13 KJV)

Firstly, "darkness" is often used in the scriptures to signify ignorance and especially that ignorance of God and godliness into which all men have been cast, by the transgression of our first parent. Used in that sense, it denotes that absolute, complete ignorance of everything spiritual, heavenly, and divine, that black and gloomy cloud of worse than midnight, deeper than Egyptian darkness, which broods so thickly and settles so densely over the minds of men.

Thus the prophet speaks - "Darkness shall cover the earth and thick darkness the people" (Isaiah 60:2). And again - "The people that walked in darkness have seen a great light – those who dwell in the land of the shadow of death, upon them has the light shined" (Isaiah 9:2 KJV). So also – "And the light shines in darkness, and the darkness comprehended it not" (John 1:5 AKJV).

In all these passages – and there are many more such in scripture – the word "darkness" is used to signify that dense ignorance which broods over the minds of men, so that they cannot see or know, understand or feel anything of the power of God's truth. Well has David described their state, "They know not, neither will they understand; they walk on in darkness" (Psalms 82:5 AKJV).

This is the state described by the prophet as quoted by John, "Therefore they could not believe, because Elijah said again, He has blinded their eyes, and hardened their heart; that they could not see with their eyes, nor understand with their heart, and be converted, and I should heal them" (John 12:39-40 KJV). In this state all men are by nature, and in this state thousands live and die, ignorant of the only true God and Jesus Christ whom He has sent, and therefore are destitute of eternal life.

Secondly, "darkness" has in scripture another meaning – that of sin. Thus the scripture says – "Have no fellowship with the unfruitful works of darkness, but rather reprove them" (Ephesians 5:11 KJV). We know that darkness favours sin; that when the sun goes down and night covers the earth, that is the time for the sinner to creep abroad to practice his deeds of wickedness. Just as the owl, when the sun declines and the shades of night fall, comes out of her ivy tower in quest of her prey, so does the ungodly sinner come forth in the evening gloom or the midnight hour to commit, under the veil of night, those deeds that shun the light of day.

We are to "give thanks unto the Father" for all these visitations of His grace, for all these blessed manifestations of His goodness and love. Have you any hope, any inward testimony, that the Lord has by his Spirit wrought these miracles of mercy and grace in your heart? O, what thanks and praises are due to the God and Father of the Lord Jesus Christ, if He has wrought these things in our soul, for His unspeakable mercy in stretching forth His hand to save you!

Transferred us into the Kingdom of His Son

For it pleased the Father that in Him all the fullness should dwell, and by Him to reconcile all things to Himself, by Him, whether things on earth or things in heaven, having made peace through the blood of His cross.

And you, who once were alienated and enemies in your mind by wicked works, yet now He has reconciled in the body of His flesh through death, to present you holy, and blameless, and above reproach in His sight. If indeed you continue in the faith, grounded and steadfast, and are not moved away from the hope of the gospel which you heard, which was preached to every creature under heaven, of which I, Paul, became a minister.
(Colossians 1:19-23)

The blood of Jesus Christ has brought peace to all humanity. We were separated from God because of sin and had no acceptable offering to satisfy the demands of God's holy nature. Therefore God sent Christ Jesus to provide an acceptable sacrifice for sin, establishing a path with those who will receive Him, thereby making peace to them.

Having Made Peace Through the Blood

Jesus did not come as an accident. The blood is very important; do you know what the body is without blood? Adam and Eve sinned, God killed an animal and covered them with skin – blood was shed for their sins.

God delivered the children of Israel out of Egypt through blood sacrifice. What are the consequences of sin? Every single person needs the blood of Jesus. Let us consider the following gifts so that we can appreciate the Father at all times.

1. REDEMPTION: redemption means to buy something back. Jesus came to purchase us from slavery and sin. He came as substitute – (to serve in place of another person or thing). When we ask Jesus to forgive our sins then we have been redeemed.

> *Knowing that you were not redeemed with corruptible things, like silver or gold, from your aimless conduct received by tradition from your fathers, but with the precious blood of Christ, as of a lamb without blemish and without spot.*
>
> *(1 Peter 1:18-19)*

2. FORGIVENESS: when you were saved you asked Jesus to forgive your sins. Your forgiveness did not come because you prayed long. You were forgiven because you accepted Him as your Saviour. Jesus became your substitute.

> *In Him we have redemption (deliverance) through His blood, the forgiveness of sins, according to the riches of His grace, which He made to abound towards us in all wisdom and prudence (understanding) having made known to us the mystery of His will, according to His good pleasure which He purposed in Himself.*
> *(Ephesians 1:7-9)*

> *But as many as received Him, to them He gave the right to become children of God, to those who believe in His name.*
> *(John 1:12)*

Forgiveness is a process that only God can accomplish in us. Forgiveness is beyond us – it is the work of God in us. Therefore, we must allow God to work in us as we continue to walk with Him daily.

3. JUSTIFICATION: justification is the declaring of a person to be just or righteous. We are justified, declared righteous, at the moment of our salvation. Justification does not make us righteous, but rather pronounces us righteous.

Our righteousness comes from placing our faith in the finished work of Jesus Christ. His sacrifice covers our sin, allowing God to see us as perfect and unblemished. Because as believers we are in Christ, God sees Christ's own righteousness when He looks at us. This meets God's demands for perfection; thus, He declares us righteous – He justifies us.

Consequently, just as the result of one trespass was condemnation for all men, so also the result of one act of righteousness was justification that brings life for all men. For just as through the disobedience of the one man the many were made sinners, so also through the obedience of the one man the many will be made righteous.
(Romans 5:18-19 NIV)

It is because of justification that the peace of God can rule in our lives. It is because of justification that believers can have assurance of salvation. It is the fact of justification that enables God to begin the process of sanctification—the process by which God makes us in reality what we already are appositionally. "Therefore, since we have been justified through faith, we have peace with God through our Lord Jesus Christ" (Romans 5:1 NIV).

God is holy and has to punish sin, see Romans 6:23. God sent His Son to take our place, that is forgiveness of sin. This is a great exchange. He died for us so we can live. In Christ's righteousness we can have wisdom to see as He sees, think as He thinks and react as He reacts. "Let this mind be in you, which also was in Christ Jesus" (Philippians 2:5).

4. RECONCILIATION: reconciliation speaks of separation and coming together. God is the only One who takes initiative to come to us. When sin separated us from God, the Lord came to us through Jesus Christ. He loves us and for that matter He reconciles with us. The scripture says, we love Him because He first loved us (1 John 4:19).

For it pleased the Father that in Him all the fullness should dwell, and by Him to reconcile all things to Himself, by

> *Him, whether things on earth or things in heaven, having made peace through the blood of His cross. And you, who once were alienated and enemies in your mind by wicked works, yet now He has reconciled in the body of His flesh through death, to present you holy, and blameless, and above reproach in His sight.*
>
> *(Colossians 1:19-22)*

5. <u>SANCTIFICATION</u>: is a period when God sets you apart. Christian living is a process; we grow into maturity step by step, in the Word of God and by yielding to the Holy Spirit. And so Jesus also suffered outside the city gate to make the people holy through his own blood (Hebrews 13:12).

In the Old Testament the Holy of Holies is where God resides. And it was only the priest who went in there. But now we can go to the Holy of Holies only through the blood of Jesus.

> *Therefore, brothers and sisters, since we have confidence to enter the Most Holy Place by the blood of Jesus, by a new and living way opened for us through the curtain, that is, his body.*
>
> *(Hebrews 10:19-20 NIV)*

You and I can go to the Father through the blood of Jesus. If the blood of Jesus is not in your life and you go to the Father – (Holy of Holies) then you are saying I am unholy but I am going to the Holy God.

> *But if we are living in the light, as God is in the light, then we have fellowship with each other, and the blood of Jesus, his Son, cleanses us from all sin. But if we confess our sins*

to him, he is faithful and just to forgive us our sins and to cleanse us from all wickedness.
(1 John 1:7, 9 NLT)

If we walk in love, the blood of Jesus continues to cleanse us from all wickedness. "My little children, these things write I unto you, that ye sin not. And if any man sin, we have an advocate with the Father, Jesus Christ the righteous: And he is the propitiation for our sins: and not for ours only, but also for the sins of the whole world" (1 John 2:1-2 KJV).

To propitiate means, sacrifice. When you and I come to Him, He makes everything possible for us. Grace is all about God's awesome forgiveness. The blood of Jesus is the only way to heaven. The blood is the only thing that gives us the permission to bring our thanksgiving to the altar of God.

A Thankful Heart

Thankfulness is foundational to the Christian life. Thankfulness is a conscious response that comes from looking beyond our blessings, to their source. As Christians, we have been forgiven, saved from death, and adopted as God's children. There could be no better reason for a grateful heart!

Lepers in Jesus' day were social outcasts. Their highly contagious condition deprived them from those they loved. These ten men had been forbidden to enter their own villages, to live in their own homes, to work in their own jobs, or even to touch their own children. Imagine what unrestrained joy must have filled them as they ran back home again!

Ten men were joyfully rushing to share the good news with those they loved. Among the ten only one considered the source of that blessing and returned to thank and worship the One who had given him back his life.

We, too, have been healed and made whole by the Saviour. We are free to enjoy the abundant life the Saviour has graciously given us. Could we, like the nine lepers, rush off so quickly to glory in our blessings without stopping to thank our Redeemer? God looks for our thanks.

> *Now it happened as He went to Jerusalem that He passed through the midst of Samaria and Galilee. Then as He entered a certain village, there met Him ten men who were lepers, who stood afar off. And they lifted up their voices and said, "Jesus, Master, have mercy on us!"*
>
> *So when He saw them, He said to them, go show yourselves to the priests. And so it was that as they went, they were cleansed. And one of them, when he saw that he was healed, returned, and with a loud voice glorified God, and fell down on his face at His feet, giving Him thanks. And he was a Samaritan. So Jesus answered and said, were there not ten cleansed? But where are the nine? Were there not any found who returned to give glory to God except this foreigner?*
>
> (Luke 17:11-17)

As God's children there must be reflections in our minds, for example, "What can I give thanks to God for right now?" Is my thankfulness to God reflected in my relationship with Him?

Give thanks to the Lord, call on his name; make known among the nations what he has done. Sing to him, sing praise to him; tell of all his wonderful acts. Glory in his holy name; let the hearts of those who seek the Lord rejoice.
(1 Chronicles 16:8-10 NIV)

Thanking God in the Midst of Affliction

One of the most important things we must do when we suffer is to give thanks. I don't say this lightly and I know many believers who have endured unimaginable pain and tragedy. Giving thanks in the midst of agony and affliction is certainly not easy to do. Yet Ephesians 5:20 tells us we should give thanks, "always and for everything to God the Father in the name of our Lord Jesus Christ" (ESV). 1 Thessalonians 5:18 says to "give thanks in all circumstances; for this is the will of God in Christ Jesus for you" (ESV)

Giving thanks helps us focus on God in our affliction, steers us away from complaining, strengthens our faith, and brings glory to Jesus.

God is always with you in your affliction "When you pass through the waters, I will be with you; and through the rivers, they shall not overwhelm you; when you walk through fire you shall not be burned, and the flame shall not consume you" (Isaiah 43:2 ESV). Remember that this affliction is momentary and light compared to the eternal reward it is producing. For this light momentary affliction is preparing for us an eternal weight of glory beyond all comparison (2 Corinthians 4:17). Jesus is your sympathetic High Priest who intercedes for you constantly.

"For we do not have a high priest who is unable to sympathize with our weaknesses, but one who in every respect has been tempted as we are, yet without sin" (Hebrews 4:15 ESV). Consequently, he is able to save to the uttermost those who draw near to God through Him, since He always lives to make intercession for them. When affliction comes you have Jesus, He is your refuge, strength, and strong tower that you can run to.

Chapter 3

Celebrating the Annual Thanksgiving and Harvest

In many churches and nations, days and periods have been set apart to commemorate feasts for thanksgiving and annual harvest. These periods of celebration are very wonderful because it's the time the entire church presents their harvest and thanks together before the Lord.

Countries like the United States of America and Canada have a nation wide thanksgiving to the Lord in the months of October and November. Many people consider Thanksgiving as a more favourable annual celebration than Christmas. Because it is a period when families, friends and loved ones come together to eat and celebrate, it is so awesome for such a day and it's good to appreciate and thank Him collectively.

But do not get me wrong, thanksgiving shouldn't be a yearly event; it should be all the time and must be a lifestyle.

Thanksgiving should be more than an end of the year feast - it should be a lifestyle. Thanksgiving is the act of giving thanks. It means keeping an attitude of gratitude toward God every day, and is a master key to seeing the fullness of God manifested in our lives.

> *Through Him, therefore, let us constantly and at all times offer up to God a sacrifice of praise, which is the fruit of lips that thankfully acknowledge and confess and glorify His name.*
>
> *(Hebrews 13:15 AMP)*

The above scripture talks about a "sacrifice" of praise. This simply means that it might be hard for us to give thanks to God at various times. The Word makes it clear, however, that we must give thanks continually — whether we feel like it or not, it should be a lifestyle. Your lips or mouth should produce fruits of thanksgiving daily.

Every believer should present a sacrifice of praise, at all times, for what the Lord has done. Our praise and thanksgiving comes through Him. The scripture says, through Him, therefore, let us constantly and at all times offer up to God a sacrifice of praise which is the fruit of lips. When we acknowledge what God has done through His Son, Jesus Christ for us, confession of thankfulness must proceed from our mouth.

Thanksgiving must be cultivated. To *cultivate* means "to improve by labour, to refine." This means that thanksgiving doesn't happen automatically; we are going to have to work at it. We must practice giving thanks all the time—not just in church or wait until the year comes to an end it should be all the time, at every place, at home, at work, and even when we are stuck in rush-hour traffic!

Wherever we are, we are to offer spoken words of thanks to help cultivate a spirit and atmosphere of thanksgiving. This continual praise will position us to experience fullness in our lives. *Fullness* means "nothing needed, nothing wanted."

> *Thank [God] in everything [no matter what the circumstances may be, be thankful and give thanks], for this is the will of God for you [who are] in [the Anointed] Jesus [the Revealer and Mediator of that will].*
> *(1 Thessalonians 5:18 AMP)*

This scripture says we are to thank God in everything. In everything means bad or good times. If we cultivate an attitude or lifestyle of thanksgiving to the Lord, we must in every situation refuse to murmur or complain and instead glorify Him and believe Him for a way of escape.

Be Thankful Even if you are in Difficult Circumstances

Giving thanks in difficult situations implies of having faith. There was a time in 2012, when one of our local branches had armed robbers invade the auditorium and take away all our instruments, heating systems and left us with nothing. Members gathered together and prayed and wept before the Lord. After the corporate prayer of the church, I shared a page of scripture by thanking the Lord in all things and prayed for those who had come to steal those items.

As soon as the meeting was over some of the desperate members came to me and asked why I thanked the Lord and also prayed for such evil acts. They said that I should have cursed them and shouldn't have even thanked the Lord in such an unpleasant situation.

I then comforted them again and showed them this scripture – "Thank God in everything, no matter what the circumstances may be…" (1 Thessalonians 5:18 AMP) and, "Repay no one evil for evil, but take thought for what is honest and proper and noble [aiming to be above reproach] in the sight of everyone. Do not let yourself be overcome by evil, but overcome (master) evil with good" (Romans 12:17, 21 AMP).

We are the sons of the light, we don't have to curse those who spitefully use us and persecute us. We know that when we pray to our Father, He will fight for us. He says to us, "Do not say, I will repay evil; wait [expectantly] for the Lord, and He will rescue you" (Proverbs 20:22 AMP).

Sometimes it is not easy to say all this especially when you are in a hot situation but that is what the Word of God says. Thanking God in difficult circumstances builds up your faith. By thanking Him, you trust Him to turn the situation around.

How to Develop a Lifestyle of Thanksgiving

Take time to thank God for each member of the family He has given you. Then pick three individuals from your list to whom you can express gratitude today, either in person, by phone, or by means of a note. (You may want to express gratitude to someone on your list who has been especially difficult to love!)

Make a list of other individuals who have blessed or touched your life in some way. You may want to include pastors, teachers, friends, business associates, neighbours, authors, leaders of Christian ministries, etc. As you write each name, ask yourself, "Have I ever thanked that person for the way God has used him/her in my life?"

Put a check mark next to each individual to whom you have expressed gratitude. Call or write three people on the list you made yesterday, to express your gratitude for their influence and ministry in your life.

Paul is writing to the church in Corinth to make plans to pick up the money that they have collected to help the church in Judea during a time of famine. Paul has heard that the Corinthians have collected a large sum of money, and he is praising the church for their generosity. It is during this praise that Paul writes the famous line, "God loves a cheerful giver" (2 Corinthians 9:7).

At the end of this passage, Paul reminds the Corinthians that God will bless them for their generosity and that also, God will be praised because of their generosity.

He who supplies seed to the sower and bread for food will supply and multiply your seed for sowing and increase the harvest of your righteousness. You will be enriched in every way for all your generosity, which through us will produce thanksgiving to God.

> *For the ministry of this service is not only supplying the needs of the saints, but is also overflowing in many thanksgivings to God. By their approval of this service, they will glorify God because of your submission flowing from your confession of the gospel of Christ, and the generosity of your contribution for them and for all others, while they long for you and pray for you, because of the surpassing grace of God upon you. Thanks be to God for his inexpressible gift!*
>
> *(2 Corinthians 9:10-15 ESV)*

So, in 2 Corinthians 9:12, Paul is saying that the Corinthian's monetary offering (collected in order to help God's people in Judea) is a priestly work, which meets the needs of the saints. But this service to others, which is actually priestly service to God, doesn't only meet the needs of God's people; it also results in thanksgiving to God. In fact, Paul says their service (giving money, in this case) is abundant with many thanksgivings (plural) to God.

If we continue reading to the end of chapter nine, we see that the Corinthian's service results in thanksgiving to God, the reception by the believers in Judea results in thanksgiving to God, and Paul himself offers thanks to God.

The clear and abundant principle here is that our service to others results in the abundance of many thanksgivings to God on many different levels and by many different people. So in essence thanksgiving becomes a lifestyle to all people. Both Christians and non Christians because God's Word teaches that we should do good to all people. God Himself does well to all mankind, He gives rain, air, water, sun, heat cold and so forth, to all living things, because He is good.

But Who am I?

King David acknowledged that he is nobody before the Lord. All that he could do, all that he had acquired were by the grace of the Lord, God. So he blessed the Lord at all times:

*Therefore David blessed the LORD before all the assembly; and David said: "Blessed are You, LORD God of Israel, our Father, forever and ever. Yours, O LORD, **is** the greatness, The power and the glory, The victory and the **majesty**; For all **that is** in heaven and in earth **is Yours**; Yours is the kingdom, O LORD, And You are exalted as head over all. Both riches and honor **come** from You, And You reign over all. In Your hand is power and might; In Your hand **it is** to make great And to give strength to all. Now therefore, our God, We thank You And praise Your glorious name."*
(1 Chronicles 29:10-13 ESV)

In verse fourteen of the passage David asked himself a question **"but who am I?"** by knowing who you are before the Lord, God Almighty will help you to honour and fear Him.

But who am I, and who are my people, That we should be able to offer so willingly as this? For all things come from You, And of Your own we have given You.
(1 Chronicles 29:14)

David declared the majesty of the Lord. Majesty in the passage means, glory, honour, and beauty, excellence in form and appearance – that means God is splendour and glory.

David is saying – everything that exists is from You, and we administer it from Your hand.

We owe nothing in this world. God is the fountainhead of all life and power; man is the appointed heir for its management. "The heavens are yours, and the earth is yours; everything in the world is yours - you created it all (Psalms 89:11 NLT). It is God only who identifies Himself as, "I AM WHO I AM." Revealing His divine name declares His character and attributes, reinforcing that the issue is not who we are, but who is with Him - the God of heaven and earth.

David acknowledged the goodness of the Lord after building the Temple and offering for thanksgiving. That's the reason why he said, "but who am I, and who *are* my people, That we should be able to offer so willingly as this? For all things *come* from You, And of Your own we have given You" (1 Chronicles 29:14), because He alone is worthy of, "I AM WHO I AM" (see Exodus chapter three).

To obey is better than sacrifice and to love God and our neighbour better than all burnt-offerings. **God demands the heart, and how can human inventions please Him, when repentance, faith, and holiness are neglected?** We must acknowledge Him in all our ways, depend upon His wisdom, power, and goodness, and refer ourselves wholly to Him, and so give Him glory. Thus we must keep up communion with God; meeting Him with prayers under trials, and with praises in deliverances. A believing supplicant shall not only be graciously answered as to his petition, and so we have cause for praising God, but shall also have grace to praise Him.

Celebrating the Annual Thanksgiving and Harvest

The Law of Seedtime and Harvest

Noah's obedience to God kept him and his family from the great flood. The Word of God says that Noah was a just man, perfect in his generation and, walked with God (Genesis 6:9). After the flood, Noah built an alter to the Lord and offered Him gratitude for his deliverance.

> *Then Noah built an altar to the LORD, and took of every clean animal and of every clean bird, and offered burnt offerings on the altar. And the LORD smelled a soothing aroma. Then the LORD said in His heart,*
>
> *"I will never again curse the ground for man's sake, although the imagination of man's heart is evil from his youth; nor will I again destroy every living thing as I have done. While the earth remains, seedtime and harvest, cold and heat, winter and summer, and day and night shall not cease."*
>
> *(Genesis 8:20-22 ESV)*

We see through the scriptures that there is no direct command specifically instructing Noah to offer a blood sacrifice, he did it out of his heart. Noah's sacrifice was pleasing to God, and in response, God covenanted not to destroy creation again by flood. Your obedience and thanksgiving towards God can bring blessings to others.

After the flood the law of seedtime and harvest came into being. When God created the first living thing, He gave it the ability to grow and multiply, through the seed. Every life began by the seed principle. The flood brought a curse upon the ground, therefore, before mankind could cultivate harvest he needed to sow the seed. If men fail to sow seed they cannot harvest. "While the earth remains, seedtime and harvest, shall not cease" (Genesis 8:20-22).

People have Reasons not to Give to the Lord

Whoever gives from the heart will be blessed by the Lord. "Now may He (God) who supplies seed to the sower, and bread for food, supply and multiply the seed you have sown and increase the fruit of your righteousness" (2 Corinthians 9:10).

> *They do not say in their heart, let us now fear the Lord our God, who gives rain, both the former and the latter, in its season. He reserves for us the appointed weeks of the harvest.*
>
> *(Jeremiah 5:24)*

They did not acknowledge the Lord, they did not appreciate Him, and they failed to give thanks. Failing to honour God is sin, it is an act of ingratitude. Jesus was not happy with the other nine lepers who failed to come to Him with their thanks.

> *I will take away their harvest, declares the Lord. There will be no grapes on the vine. There will be no figs on the tree, and their leaves will wither. What I have given them will be taken from them.*
>
> *(Jeremiah 8:13 NIV)*

> *The harvest is past, the summer has ended, and we are not saved.*
>
> *(Jeremiah 8:20 NIV)*

In this passage of the scripture the prophet travails for the nation of Israel. The people of Israel are depicted as a grape that has been cut off from the vine. People failed to give to the Lord at the harvest time. They have not come to the knowledge that it's God who gives them the plentiful harvest.

Because they failed to believe and trust that it is the Lord who provides for their harvest, they live in fear that when harvest is over they would not survive, "The harvest is past, the summer has ended, and we are not saved." If people fail to trust that God is the supplier of all things and that He is the one who supplies seed to the sower and bread for food, then they will always live in fear and insecurity.

In the book of Deuteronomy, God set up a period for the Israelites to celebrate, "The Festival of Weeks." God had commanded them that before they enjoy their harvest they should count seven weeks from the time they put the sickle (cutlass) to the grain. From the seventh week of harvest they should appear before the Lord with thanksgiving. In other words before they finished their harvest, they should come before Him with a freewill offering according to the blessing of the Lord upon their lives. This offering is an offering of appreciation and thanksgiving for His faithfulness.

As they come before the Lord in celebration with joy they give their gratitude of great deliverance from bondage in Egypt. All Christians must be reminded that they were also once in Egypt (the world) and the Lord delivered them from the bondages of sin and death.

Count off seven weeks from the time you begin to put the sickle to the standing grain. Then celebrate the Festival of Weeks to the Lord your God by giving a freewill offering in proportion to the blessings the Lord your God has given you.

And rejoice before the Lord your God at the place he will choose as a dwelling for his Name – you, your sons and daughters, your male and female servants, the Levites in your towns, and the foreigners, the fatherless and the widows living among you. Remember that you were slaves in Egypt, and follow carefully these decrees.
(Deuteronomy 16:9-12 NIV)

Again they are to keep, "The Festival of Tabernacles," this is a festival seven days after they have gathered the produce of their threshing-floor and winepress. This period of agriculture year is just to appreciate God for His goodness and mercy. In this feast they rejoiced for their freedom, deliverance, abundance etc.

God asked the men to appear before Him three times a year with a gift, according to each one's blessings. Now we the New Testament believers cannot overlook what the Lord has done for us, we are the most privileged, therefore, our thanksgiving and harvest should not be periodical but all the time – it should be a lifestyle.

We should emulate from the people of old. "Three times a year all your men must appear before the Lord your God at the place he will choose: at the Festival of Unleavened Bread, the Festival of Weeks and the Festival of Tabernacles. No one should appear before the Lord empty-handed: Each of you must bring a gift in proportion to the way the Lord your God has blessed you" (Deuteronomy 16:16-17 NIV).

> *Celebrate the Festival of Tabernacles for seven days after you have gathered the produce of your threshing floor and your winepress. Be joyful at your festival — you, your sons and daughters, your male and female servants, and the Levites, the foreigners, the fatherless and the widows who live in your towns. For seven days celebrate the festival to the Lord your God at the place the Lord will choose. For the Lord your God will bless you in all your harvest and in all the work of your hands, and your joy will be complete.*
>
> *(Deuteronomy 16:13-15 NIV)*

Harvest Time

Harvesting is the gathering of crops, the season when ripened crops are gathered or a supply of anything gathered at maturity and stored – harvest wheat. So in essence, harvesting is to gain, acquire or is the result of any past act, process, plant etc. Harvesting is not necessarily agriculture because the book of Galatians says, "…for whatever a man sows, that he will also reap" (Galatians 6:7). If you sow peace, you will harvest peace, if you sow love, you will reap love. You will harvest anything that you have sown in life, whether a good or bad seed; know for sure that there is a harvest time!

> *And He said, "The kingdom of God is as if a man should scatter seed on the ground, and should sleep by night and rise by day, and the seed should sprout and grow, he*

himself does not know how. For the earth yields crops by itself: first the blade, then the head, after that the full grain in the head. But when the grain ripens, immediately he puts in the sickle, because the harvest has come.

(Mark 4:26-29)

There is time for sowing and a time for gathering. God in the season of gathering is going to help you. In the above passage of scripture, we will now consider six principles regarding sowing and reaping.

First: seed – a seed is the productive source. If you are going to harvest, you must have a seed. The seed is the original intent of the harvest. God is the supplier of the seed.

Second: soil – the seed functions within the environment. Many times God gives us seeds but the soil we plant matters a lot. If you are going to gather a bountiful crop of harvest then you must acquire a proper environment, the soil or ground.

Third: scattering – in this passage, Jesus did not say, we should plant the seed but scatter. That means throw the seeds, scattering them. This speaks of generosity without discrimination; don't withhold your seed or money. The book of Ecclesiastes chapter 11:1 says, "Cast your bread upon the waters, for you will find it after many days."

This scripture also speaks of generosity and investment. The liberal person will be rich. Don't hoard your money or seed. Simply be generous with your wealth. Scattering means continue to sow at all times, at any giving opportunity because you don't know which seed will bring the harvest.

Fourth: sleep – is the waiting period. We all sleep in the night and wake up by the day. The sleep that Jesus is saying here is not just being negligent but He is saying that when you sow you need to wait for the gathering. When I was about the age of seven a family friend gave me a coconut seed. I planted it and waited for about two months and I did not a see any sign of it germinating, so I decided to dig to see why it has been kept so long. With impatience, I broke the blade and the coconut died.

Fifth: sprouting – is the result. The farmer does not control the growth. It is the work of God – nature. Man is responsible for sowing but only God can produce. In this essence, Jesus talks about three levels of results that bring about growth.

1. The **blade:** example, before you harvest a full grain of corn, you first see the blade. The blade tells you that something good is coming. You do not harvest the blade. When God begins to show you the blade, you need patience. You allow it to mature. You don't consume the blade.

2. The **head:** when God shows you the head you don't harvest. You wait until it becomes a full grain. Many times when people see a little turnover of their business or small percentage of their profit they squander it and finally run into debt.

3. The **full grain:** the sower or the farmer must wait for the full grain. The full grain is in the head – harvest. The full grain is the mature crop.

Sixth: sickle – a sickle is a harvest instrument, a cutting machine. Jesus said, as soon as the harvest is ready, the sickle must be applied. Without the sickle, the harvest can be wasted. Many times, we have the seed and the soil we scatter and produce but at the harvest time, we are not prepared. Without proper preparation, the whole effort of scattering would be unprofitable.

Then He said to His disciples, the harvest truly is plentiful, but the laborers are few. Therefore pray the Lord of the harvest to send out laborers into His harvest.
(Matthew 9:37-38)

The harvest is ready but the labourers are few. The sowing capacity is always lower than the gathering. The work force of a harvest is always greater. For example, if one person can plant a field of a corn one day, the person can use one week to gather up the crop. So in principle, whoever sows seed must be fully prepared for the bountiful harvest. In other words when you give, be ready for the harvest; put much effort to plan well to gather the harvest.

The kingdom of God is as if a man should scatter seed on the ground, and should sleep by night and rise by day, and the seed should sprout and grow, he himself does not know how. For the earth yields crops by itself: first the blade, then the head, after that the full grain in the head. But when the grain ripens, immediately he puts in the sickle, because the harvest has come.
(Mark 4:26-29)

What does the Term Firstfruit mean in the Bible?

Firstfruit is a term used in the bible to describe the firstfruit of the first harvest. God commanded His people to present the firstfruit of the land to the Levitical priesthood (Deuteronomy 26:2). Since Levites did not receive any land when the children of Israel received their inheritance in Canaan, God provided a way for them to be supported through the others tribes.

Honour the LORD with thy substance and with the firstfruits of all thine increase.
(Proverbs 3:9 KJV)

God commanded ancient Israel to offer the firstfruit of their harvest to Him in gratitude of the blessings they received (Exodus 23:19; 34:26; Ezekiel 44:30; etc.)

The firstfruit of a harvest plays an important role in the celebrating of God's annual feast days. On the day after the weekly Sabbath during the festive season known as the Days of Unleavened Bread, the priest waved barley before God (Leviticus 23:9-11).

On the day of Pentecost (which is also known as the Feast of Firstfruits), fifty days later, two loaves made of fine flour were waved before God as His offering (Leviticus 23:17, 20). This marked the end of the grain (first) harvest and the beginning of the fruit harvest in Israel. On the first day of the Feast of Tabernacles in the fall, Israel was commanded to offer the first of their produce and juices to Him (Exodus 22:29 see also Numbers 18:12-13).

When we come into the New Testament, Pentecost takes on a deeper spiritual meaning. Pentecost becomes the "birthday" of the New Testament church as God gives His Holy Spirit, with signs and wonders (Acts 2:1-4).

All people who are truly called out of this world, who have repented of their sins and have in them God's Holy Spirit, are considered by the Father to be His firstfruits of the salvation of man.

The Firstfruits

The firstfruits are the first harvest that is gathered in a harvest. In scripture God asked the children of Israel to bring their first produce as thanksgiving offering, this firstfruit is appreciation to God as the Lord of the harvest. "The harvest truly is plentiful, but the laborers are few. Therefore pray the Lord of the harvest to send out laborers into His harvest" (Matthew 9:37-38). The bible depicts farmers in a very positive way; they are people with natural faith. They sow seed and wait patiently for the early and later rain for a bumper crop. They do not know how the seed grows and matures, they believe the natural law that governs the seed and harvest time.

We Christians know that our God is the Lord of the harvest. Scripture teaches that the Word of God is a seed, see Matthew 13. In first Corinthians 3, Paul reminds us that God is the One who brings the increase or the harvest therefore, no flesh – should boast of anything they possessed. "Who then is Paul, and who is Apollos, but ministers through whom you believed, as the Lord gave to each one? **I planted,**

Apollos watered, but God gave the increase. So then neither he who plants is anything, nor he who waters, but God who gives the increase" (1 Corinthians 3:5-7).

In our church the Firstfruits Feast or the Firstfruits Day is the period that the church collectively comes together to appreciate the Lord for giving Jesus Christ as the firstfruit of the saints and we also who have the firstfruits of the Spirit (Romans 8:23).

In this period the entire church comes before God with seed of income to express our thanks before Him. Sometimes people come with different kinds of fruits as the Old Testament people brought their firstfruits before God, we then pray over them and share, as to remember the goodness of the Lord.

But now Christ is risen from the dead, and has become the firstfruits of those who have fallen asleep. For since by man came death, by Man also came the resurrection of the dead. For as in Adam all die, even so in Christ all shall be made alive. But each one in his own order: Christ the firstfruits, afterward those who are Christ's at His coming.
(1 Corinthians 15:20-23)

The Firstfruits is Symbolic of God's Harvest of Souls

The Firstfruits was a Jewish feast held in the early spring at the beginning of the grain harvest. We must understand that the Old Testament is the fulfilment of the New Testament. Everything that happened in the Old was a shadow of the

New. We shouldn't forget that Jesus said "I came to fulfill the law, and not even one jot of the law will be taken away until all is fulfilled" (see Matthew 5:18).

The firstfruits speaks of thanksgiving, acknowledgment, reverence and partnership with God.

> *When you have come into the land that the Lord your God is giving you as an inheritance to possess, and you possess it, and settle in it, you shall take some of the first of all the fruit of the ground, which you harvest from the land that the Lord your God is giving you, and you shall put it in a basket and go to the place that the Lord your God will choose as a dwelling for his name.*
>
> *You shall go to the priest who is in office at that time, and say to him, "Today I declare to the Lord your God that I have come into the land that the Lord swore to our ancestors to give us." When the priest takes the basket from your hand and sets it down before the altar of the Lord your God, you shall make this response before the Lord your God: "A wandering Aramean was my ancestor; he went down into Egypt and lived there as an alien, few in number, and there he became a great nation, mighty and populous. When the Egyptians treated us harshly and afflicted us, by imposing hard labour on us, we cried to the Lord, the God of our ancestors; the Lord heard our voice and saw our affliction, our toil, and our oppression.*
>
> *The Lord brought us out of Egypt with a mighty hand and an outstretched arm, with a terrifying display of power, and with signs and wonders; and he brought us into this*

place and gave us this land, a land flowing with milk and honey. So now I bring the first of the fruit of the ground that you, O Lord, have given me." You shall set it down before the Lord your God and bow down before the Lord your God.

(Deuteronomy 26:1-10 NRSV)

This passage deals with one's attitude in giving an offering of firstfruits and the tithe. It teaches that both should be given with an attitude of joyful worship, as a testimony to God's personal provision and deliverance. In 1 Corinthians 16:2, Paul taught us to give on the first day of the week just as the offering of the firstfruits was an occasion of thanksgiving, so that the Christian is to give with gladness. In the New Testament the firstfruit offering mentioned seven times - always symbolically – refers to the first believers, as firstfruits.

In summary, firstfruits symbolize God's harvest of souls. We need to win souls to the kingdom of God. Therefore we must trust God with our firstfruits or income, to preach the gospel.

Harvest and Reapers

The Lord Jesus Christ asked us to pray to the Father to send reapers because the harvest is plentiful. A reaper is a farming tool or person that reaps or cuts and gathers crop at harvest, when they are ripe. It would be a waste if a farmer spent time, money and effort to cultivate land but does not hire reapers to harvest the crop. Harvest time is an important period for all those who have sown, because the harvest involves all efforts made. Harvest is a reward or profit time.

Jesus Christ declares that no time should be wasted when the harvest is ready.

> *Do you not say, "There are still four months and then comes the harvest"? Behold, I say to you, lift up your eyes and look at the fields, for they are already white for harvest! And he who reaps receives wages, and gathers fruit for eternal life, that both he who sows and he who reaps may rejoice together. For in this the saying is true: "One sows and another reaps." I sent you to reap that for which you have not labored; others have labored, and you have entered into their labors.*
>
> *(John 4:35-38)*

The Gospel is a Seed

Christians are like farmers, we sow and we preach the Good News of Jesus Christ. The world is the field. The people are the harvest. The workers of the kingdom are the reapers. We are commissioned to spread the gospel as a seed to the ends of the field – the world. When a person hears the gospel of Jesus and takes it to heart, and goes on to spread the gospel further with good deeds and Christlike love, they are like "good soil" from which a planted seed sprouts into a beautiful plant. Through the Good News, that forgiveness and eternal life are given freely based on the death, burial, and resurrection of our Lord Jesus Christ, the Son of the Living God.

The Five Good Soils you can Sow

I encourage ministers with genuine God-given visions to trust that God will provide the necessary resources to carry out their visions. The resources God provides must be used to further His kingdom and reach out to the poor, orphans and widows. Every believer must have in mind that God requires them to give generously. There are five soils a believer can sow a seed for a bumper harvest:

1. The poor and the needy
2. The orphans
3. The widows
4. The kingdom of God/church and evangelism
5. The minister of the gospel

Let us first make it our goal to seek the face of the Lord more than we seek His hands. Let us also be faithful in the little He has entrusted to us. Then when financial increase comes, we will be able to correctly appropriate it for the vision He has given us. When You said, "Seek My face," My heart said to You, "Your face, Lord, I will seek" (Psalms 27:8).

Stop giving to the rich, "The rich rules over the poor, And the borrower is servant to the lender" (Proverbs 22:7). "He who oppresses the poor to increase his riches, And he who gives to the rich, will surely come to poverty" (Proverbs 22:16). The law of sowing and reaping is a kingdom law which, consequently, governs the earth and all natural matters.

Poverty or lack of any kind is not a money problem. It's a spiritual problem that came on mankind through the curse of sin, and it can only be solved by a revelation of what Jesus Christ did about it on the cross. It can only be conquered by renewing your mind to the fact that, "For ye know the grace of our Lord Jesus Christ, that, though he was rich, yet for your sakes he became poor, that ye through his poverty might be rich" (2 Corinthians 8:9 KJV).

During this season of Thanksgiving let us join king David in giving thanks to the God of Abraham, Isaac and Jacob for He is good and His mercies endure forever! Whether you are standing on the mountain top or walking through a deep valley, the Word of God teaches the believer to give thanks to the Lord in all things.

> *Shout for joy to the Lord, all the earth. Worship the Lord with gladness; come before Him with joyful songs. Know that the Lord is God. It is He who made us, and we are His; we are His people, the sheep of His pasture.*
>
> *Enter His gates with thanksgiving and His courts with praise; give thanks to Him and praise His name. For the Lord is good and His love endures forever; His faithfulness continues all generations.*
>
> *(Psalms 100 NIV)*

"So we, Your people and sheep of Your pasture, Will give You thanks forever; We will show forth Your praise to all generations" (Psalms 79:13).

CHAPTER 4

Dealing With Ingratitude

Ingratitude is a sin. Ingratitude is an integral part of society. Moses advised the children of Israel that they shouldn't forget what the Lord has done for them. How God delivered them from slavery, kept them forty years in the wilderness, fed them with angels food, manna and led them with a mighty hand to their promised Land. "When you have eaten and are full, then you shall bless the Lord your God for the good land which He has given you" (Deuteronomy 8:10).

We must all take heed not to forget the Lord's goodness. As human beings, sometimes when things work out alright, people forget the goodness of the Lord. You cannot enjoy the blessings and forget the One who blesses.

Lest – when you have eaten and are full, and have built beautiful houses and dwell in them; and when your herds and your flocks multiply, and your silver and your gold are multiplied, and all that you have is multiplied; when your heart is lifted up, and you forget the Lord your God who brought you out of the land of Egypt, from the house of bondage; who led you through that great and terrible wilderness, in which were fiery serpents and scorpions and thirsty land where there was no water; who brought water for you out of the flinty rock.

(Deuteronomy 8:12-15)

If you cannot remember anything that the Lord has done for you, you shouldn't forget your salvation. All Christians have been rescued from Egypt, a type of the world. It's through the mighty hands of the Lord that you and I have been saved. We were called out of the world into His marvellous kingdom. Therefore, we shouldn't forget ourselves, but rather, look to our present freedom through our past.

You cannot count the blessings the good Father has bestowed on you. The scripture says, "The blessing of the Lord makes one rich and He adds no sorrow with it" (Proverbs 10:22).

Thanksgiving should be a natural state of a man, mankind shouldn't be unthankful. Apart from the grace of God active in a man's life, there is a noticeable absence of human thanksgiving. The Word of God says, "Because although they knew God, they did not glorify Him as God" (Romans 1:21). All people know in their hearts that God exists. Creation declares His invisible attributes so men have no excuse to deny the existence of God. Lack of thankfulness is a heart problem, people know that there is a supreme God but their hearts are darkened, making them empty and vain so that they couldn't honour God.

> *Because, although they knew God, they did not glorify Him as God, nor were thankful, but became futile (useless) in their thoughts, and their foolish hearts were darkened.*
> *(Romans 1:21)*

> *But mark this: There will be terrible times in the last days. People will be lovers of themselves, lovers of money, boastful, proud, abusive, disobedient to their parents, ungrateful, unholy, without love, unforgiving, slanderous, without self-control, brutal, not lovers of the good, treacherous, rash, conceited, lovers of pleasure rather than lovers of God – having a form of godliness but denying its power. Have nothing to do with such people.*
> *(2 Timothy 3:1-5 NIV)*

Unthankfulness is so engrained in the sin darkened heart, both regenerate and unregenerate, genuine thanksgiving requires diligent attention and hard work.

> *Rejoice always, pray without ceasing, in everything give thanks; for this is the will of God in Christ Jesus for you.*
> *(1 Thessalonians 5:16-18)*

> *I thank my God upon every remembrance of you, always in every prayer of mine making request for you all with joy, for your fellowship in the gospel from the first day*

until now, being confident of this very thing, that He who has begun a good work in you will complete it until the day of Jesus Christ.

(Philippians 1:3-6)

The above text teaches some very interesting thoughts concerning thankfulness that we would be well to observe both at Thanksgiving and throughout the year.

Firstly, thanksgiving arises from joy in the work of God. "Rejoice always," comes from Paul's lips despite the challenges of life, he was in prison. He has spoken of joy in each time reflecting the joy he personally received seeing God's hand at work among the Thessalonian and Philippian believers. Real thanksgiving begins with a view of the work God is doing around you. You must take time to observe His handiwork.

Secondly, thanksgiving arises from fellowship with God in prayer. This requires a constant sense of personal dependant upon Almighty One.

Thirdly, thanksgiving arises from a keen sense of anticipation that God will continue to work on your behalf.

Paul expresses his great love and thanksgiving for these believers, as is evident from the joy, confidence and affection with which he thanks God for them. With joy apostle Paul expresses the emotions that accompany his prayers, first mentioning joy. He rejoices because of partnership, that the believers join in the work of the gospel, which includes financially supporting him.

Power to get Wealth

The word "power" in the Strong's #3581 is *"roach,"* it means capacity, vigour, strength, wealth, force, means, power or substance. In Deuteronomy chapter eight Moses informs Israel that it is God who gives to them the ability to obtain wealth. The word, "wealth" is a combination of God's blessings: mental, physical and spiritual. Your heart attitude determines your appreciation toward God. Moses reminded Israel that they shouldn't come to a conclusion that it is by their own power or strength they have obtained wealth but God's.

Power is the supernatural ability to accomplish anything in life. Power is God's anointing to carry out any task or business.

Then you say in your heart, "My power and might of my hand have gained me this wealth." And you shall remember the LORD your God, for it is He who gives you <u>power</u> to get wealth, that He may establish (confirm) His covenant which He swore to your fathers, as it is this day.
(Deuteronomy 8:17-18)

The above passage tells us that wealth should exist to confirm and verify covenant, because God wants our needs to be met and to satisfy our heart's desires. In this case you shouldn't be selfish but rather the blessing you have would be a help for others. You don't have to de squandered selfishly. As the Lord told Abraham, "I will make you a great nation; I will bless you and make your name great; and you shall be a blessing" (Genesis 12:2).

Our Salvation Cost God a Lot

If we cannot remember anything God has done for us we shouldn't forget our salvation. Our salvation and the life of the innocent Son of God, Jesus Christ. The Psalmist recorded the suffering death of Christ.

My God, My God, why have You forsaken Me? Why are You so far from helping Me, and from the words of My groaning? O My God, I cry in the daytime, but You do not hear; and in the night season, and am not silent.
(Psalms 22:1-2)

In this text, we see God Himself turning away from His beloved Son who is bearing the sin of the world. He bore our judgment and shame, our judgment brought separation from God. At that moment Jesus Christ is experiencing the darkest hour of His life, and bore it – for us.

All humanity owes God a great debt of gratitude. Therefore, thanksgiving should be a way of lifestyle. Failing to thank Him on a daily bases is the act of ingratitude. As I have said earlier, our redemption, justification, forgiveness, reconciliation, sanctification etc., is a gift from God.

Give to the Lord, O families of the peoples, Give to the Lord glory and strength. Give to the Lord the glory due His name; Bring an offering, and come before Him. Oh, worship the Lord in the beauty of holiness!
(1 Chronicles 16:28-29)

How do we Deal with People who Continually show Ingratitude?

Ingratitude is an integral part of society. If you ask most people if they are ungrateful, they will probably reply, "Of course not!" However, this attitude is so ingrained in their lives, they cannot openly admit - or even realize - that they are ungrateful.

But how can you tell if *you* are ungrateful? Are there things that identify ingratitude and if so, what can you do about it?

Webster's Dictionary defines "ingratitude" as: "forgetfulness of, or poor return for, kindness received." It can also be defined as not appreciating or valuing what you have, or have been given. **Unexpressed gratitude is also ingratitude!**

> *Every good gift and every perfect gift is from above, coming down from the Father of lights with whom there is no variation or shadow due to change.*
> *(James 1:17 ESV)*

> *Therefore let us be grateful for receiving a kingdom that cannot be shaken, and thus let us offer to God acceptable worship, with reverence and awe, for our God is a consuming fire.*
> *(Hebrews 12:28-29 ESV)*

We should never treat someone in a way we would not want to be treated. Just because someone may mistreat us, we have no right to mistreat him or her. God says vengeance is His, simply because He alone can carry out righteous justice. In fact, when we overcome evil with good, it makes an impression on those who mistreat us!

> *Therefore, whatever you want men to do to you, do also to them, for this is the Law and the Prophets.*
> *(Matthew 7:12)*

Whenever possible, we should try to avoid confrontations. If we have to be present, then we should say as few words as possible. The last thing we need to do is provoke someone. Even Christ walked away from situations that were getting out of hand (Mark 3:6-7).

Regardless of how others treat us, we are to try to have peaceful relationships with them. In the beatitudes, Jesus Christ - the Prince of Peace - said that those who are peacemakers will be called the children of God (Matthew 5:9).

> *He who has knowledge spares his words, and a man of understanding is of a calm spirit. Even a fool is counted wise when he holds his peace; when he shuts his lips, he is considered perceptive.*
> *(Proverbs 17:27-28)*

Why you Should Praise the Lord

God has been very good to us. He has given us good jobs, good food, and roofs over our heads. He has given us loving families and a church home where we can worship Him. Most importantly, He has given His Son to be a sacrifice, so our sins can be forgiven, and so that we can have a chance to go to heaven to be with Him.

Prayer of thanksgiving should be in the mouth of every husband or wife. We all must continually say, "Thank you, Father, for the gift of my spouse. You are the giver of all good and perfect blessings, and I'm amazed how You show Your love through her/him. Please help me to cherish such an amazing gift.

Please give my spouse a growing love for others in all that she/he does. Show her/him how to be Christ's ambassador in the world and to be a woman/man defined by love so that others may glorify You."

It is because of such love, we share the gospel with everyone. If husband and wife praise God for each other and pray for one another, our homes would reflect the inexpressible love of God.

Thank God for the Gift of your Local Pastor

A pastor is closely connected to the lives of the people he serves, and vicariously experiences both the joy and heartbreak that his people experience. When a young man gets married, the pastor rejoices. When the same young man gets into trouble, the pastor is heartbroken. When a couple has a child, the pastor is elated. When the same couple gets divorced five years later, the pastor is heartbroken.

Given the unique challenges of pastoral ministry, pastors desperately need encouragement. Encouragement is what keeps the pastor going. Encouragement is fuel for the pastoral engine. It's like a spiritual adrenaline shot. So how can you encourage your pastor? Here are some simple ways. Pay attention to his sermon, then, thank him for specific aspects of his sermons. Pray for him/her daily and ask God's grace, favour and direction for them.

Pay Closer Attention to His Sermon

Preaching is a funny thing. A pastor can spend anywhere between 10 to 30 hours on a sermon. This sermon prep involves prayerfully wrestling through difficult passages, figuring out how best to apply the passage to everyday life and organizing the sermon in a coherent manner. On Sunday he stands up in front of his congregation and pours himself out for forty minutes, and then it's over. Thirty hours of prep for a forty-minute sermon. And he has to do the same thing again mid-week, and the week after that, and the week after that. It's a joyful, exhausting, delightful and brutal grind.

If you want to bless your pastor, thank him very specifically for each sermon. Don't simply say, "Lovely sermon, pastor." Instead, thank him for specific phrases, specific application points, and specific ways God used the sermon to change and challenge you. This specific encouragement will echo in his mind as he prepares his next sermon. Pay close attention, then, thank your pastor specifically.

Cheerfully Support your Pastor's Leadership

This doesn't mean that you blindly support your pastor, no matter what decision he makes. It simply means that you maintain a general attitude of cheerful support toward your pastor, knowing that he is seeking to lead the church to the best of his ability, for the glory of God. I think this is the heart behind Hebrews 13:17, which says: "Obey your leaders and submit to them, for they are keeping watch over your souls, as those who will have to give an account. Let them do this with joy and not with groaning, for that would be of no advantage to you" (ESV).

Do you want your pastor to experience joy? Then cheerfully submit to his leadership. When you have the opportunity, thank your pastor for specific aspects of his leadership. Does your pastor place a strong leadership emphasis on sound doctrine? Thank him for that. Does your pastor place a strong leadership emphasis on evangelism? Thank him for that. Does your pastor place a strong leadership emphasis on mentoring others? Thank him for that and etc. You can encourage your pastor by cheerfully supporting his leadership.

Take Leadership Initiative

One of the things that constantly haunt pastors is the sense that there is always more to be done and not enough time to do it. There is more evangelism to be done, more bible studies to be started, more homebound folks to visit, more community outreach to initiate. Most pastors are burdened by all they are leaving undone.

If you want to bless the socks off of your pastor, take the initiative in ministry. Instead of asking your pastor to start more bible studies, ask your pastor if you can start a bible study. Instead of asking your pastor to create a prayer team, ask your pastor if you can start a prayer team. Instead of asking your pastor for more women's ministry, ask your pastor if you can start a women's ministry.

The work of ministry is not primarily done by pastors; it's done by the members of the church. Ephesians 4:11–12 tells us that the pastor is supposed to equip the people in his church for the work of ministry. To have more knowledge and understanding about the local ministry or ministry of helps order my book, **"Discover your Ministry in the Local Church."**

And he gave the apostles, the prophets, the evangelists, the shepherds and teachers, to equip the saints for the work of ministry, for building up the body of Christ.
(Ephesians 4:11-12 ESV)

Do you want to bless your pastor? Step up to the plate and take some initiative. Don't blame your pastor for the absence of a particular ministry. Rather, be the one who starts that ministry. Trust me: your pastor is desperate for encouragement. Pastoral ministry is often done behind the scenes, with little or no thanks. And Satan loves to discourage pastors, because few things are more dangerous than a faith-filled, thoroughly encouraged pastor. Encourage your pastor today. It's for your good and his.

Chapter 5

His Love and Promises are Forever

The bible, however, outlines some things that do last forever, and things that are temporal or perishable. Forever God will do what He has promised to do and be who He has promised to be. Time changes, situations change and life changes but the Lord is the same yesterday, today and forever. Even though He changes things and does new things, He does not change.

The essence of our thanksgiving is all about the nature of God, His Love and promises are forever. Forever the Lord will love His own. In Psalms 136, the psalmist recorded the inexpressible love of God towards His people.

Give thanks to the Lord, for he is good! His faithful love endures forever. Give thanks to the God of gods. His faithful love endures forever. Give thanks to the Lord of lords. His faithful love endures forever. Give thanks to him who alone does mighty miracles. His faithful love endures forever. Give thanks to him who made the heavens so skillfully. His faithful love endures forever. Give thanks to him who placed the earth among the waters. His faithful love endures forever.

Give thanks to him who made the heavenly lights - His faithful love endures forever. The sun to rule the day, His faithful love endures forever. And the moon and stars to rule the night His faithful love endures forever.
(Psalms 136:1-9 NLT)

Forever God will be doing what is right. "His work is honourable and glorious, and His righteousness endures forever" (Psalms 111:3). Throughout history man has established things that have not lived forever. We have kingdoms and thrones that have come and gone. Our attempts of establishing things on our own, throughout the generations have caused much detriment in our society and the world we live in.

For example, it was in God's mind to establish a king for the children of Israel forever. But the children of Israel were in haste to choose their own king as they compared themselves with other worldly kings. Whatever man does is temporal, but God's doings are forever and ever. So when the people of Israel chose king Saul, God was displeased.

Then all the elders of Israel gathered together and came to Samuel at Ramah, and said to him, "Look, you are old, and your sons do not walk in your ways. Now make us a king to judge us like all the nations." But the thing displeased

> *Samuel when they said, "Give us a king to judge us." So Samuel prayed to the Lord. And the Lord said to Samuel, "Heed the voice of the people in all that they say to you; for they have not rejected you, but they have rejected Me, that I should not reign over them."*
>
> *(1 Samuel 8:4-7)*

David was the king who was according to God's own heart, the kind of king God wanted to rule over His people. As we listen in on the promises God made to His king, we'll discover that these promises, shape the forever that God is inviting us into.

David was a teenager when the prophet Samuel anointed him to be king over Israel. Twenty-five years later David was still not ruling on the throne. Instead he had spent those years leading armies into battle and ducking from Saul's spears and living out in the wilderness and even in foreign countries. Second Samuel picks up the history of Israel immediately after Saul's death.

In chapter 2 we read that David was finally made king of Judah in the south while Ish-bosheth the son of Saul was made king of Israel in the north, a hint of the division in the kingdom that will come later. When men take the purpose and intents of God in their own hands it brings chaos and disorder. The decision that Israel took brought war, divisions and a divided kingdom.

> *Now there was a long war between the house of Saul and the house of David. But David grew stronger and stronger, and the house of Saul grew weaker and weaker.*
>
> *(2 Samuel 3:1)*

All of the people who had followed Ish-bosheth had to decide if they would accept the king that God had chosen and anointed and submit to his rule for their lives (which is really the same decision we have to make). We must all make a decision to accept the King of kings, Jesus Christ the Son of David, the Son of the Living God.

We read that, and then all the tribes of Israel came to David at Hebron and said, "Behold, we are your bone and flesh. In times past, when Saul was king over us, it was you who led out and brought in Israel. And the Lord said to you, 'You shall be shepherd of my people Israel, and you shall be prince over Israel'" (2 Samuel 5:1-3 ESV). So all the elders of Israel came to the king at Hebron, and king David made a covenant with them at Hebron before the Lord, and they anointed David king over Israel.

We see that finally David became king of all the twelve tribes of Israel. Whatever God does is forever. We see the forever King of kings, Jesus Christ in this account of the book of Samuel. In fact, the whole bible portrays Jesus Christ; God was working through David the earthly king to bring to pass the eternal King.

After David has successful and progress fully anointed three times as king to serve Israel and lead them to battles, he expressed his thanks to the Lord for His faithfulness that endures forever. "Then king David went in and sat before the Lord; and he said: Who am I, O Lord God? And what is my house, that You have brought me this far?" (2 Samuel 7:18)

The kingdom of the world has become the kingdom of our Lord and of his Christ, and he shall reign forever and ever.
(Revelation 11:15 ESV)

Thanksgiving shouldn't be a yearly activity but should be on a daily basis; it should be done 365 days a year. We have every cause to thank the Lord always. We must be thankful to God for all things including what we think are petty things, the food we eat, the new shoes, the dress, etc. Thanksgiving should be a lifestyle for every believer.

Enter into His gates with thanksgiving, and into His courts [house] with praise. Be thankful to Him, and bless His name. For the LORD is good; His mercy is everlasting, and His truth endures to all generations.
(Psalms 100:4-5)

The moment you acknowledge what the Lord has done for you, will not even wait for the yearly thanksgiving, it shall be daily acknowledgement.

King David spoke to himself, he said, "Bless the LORD, O my soul; and all that is within me, bless His holy name! Bless the LORD, O my soul, and forget not all His benefits" (Psalms 103:1-2). You see we spend time in prayer daily to ask God to do new things for us, but we have failed to thank Him for what He has done for us yesterday. **Throughout the bible any time people show gratitude, appreciation and thanksgiving to God, He always does something supernatural in their lives.**

Noah gave thanks to God after the flood – by sacrificing the best and clean animals. In Genesis chapter 9:3 God said,

"I have given you all things." We should follow the example of people like Abraham. He teaches us much about giving. He gave Lot the best land, see Genesis 13:5-18. He gave Melchizedek a tithe of all; he is the first person in the bible to show us how to give one tenth of our income to God.

> *And the king of Sodom went out to meet him after his return from the slaughter of Chedorlaomer, and of the kings that were with him, at the valley of Shaveh, which is the king's dale. And Melchizedek king of Salem brought forth bread and wine: and he was the priest of the most high God. And he blessed him, and said, blessed be Abram of the most high God, possessor of heaven and earth: And blessed be the most high God, which hath delivered thine enemies into thy hand. And he gave him tithes of all.*
>
> *And the king of Sodom said unto Abram, Give me the persons, and take the goods to thyself. And Abram said to the king of Sodom, I have lift up mine hand unto the Lord, the most high God, the possessor of heaven and earth, That I will not take from a thread even to a shoelatchet, and that I will not take any thing that is thine, lest thou shouldest say, I have made Abram rich: Save only that which the young men have eaten, and the portion of the men which went with me, Aner, Eshcol, and Mamre; let them take their portion.*
>
> *(Genesis 14:17-24 KJV)*

Abraham gave hospitality to strangers. As scripture teaches us to show hospitality to strangers. "Do not forget to show hospitality to strangers, for by so doing some people have shown hospitality to angels without knowing it" (Hebrews 13:2 NLT).

The first time God asked a man for a gift, He wanted the best - Isaac. What is a sacrifice? There are two basic principles. First, every sacrifice had to come from the personal property of the worshiper, (fish, or animal from the forest are not accepted), goat, sheep, crops and chicken were accepted. Second, only the best will do for God, (the offering had to be **"without blemish"**). "Your lamb shall be without blemish, a male a year old. You may take it from the sheep or from the goats" (Exodus 12:5 ESV).

And the Lord spoke to Moses, saying, Speak to the children of Israel, and say to them: "When you come into the land which I give to you, and reap its harvest, then you shall bring a sheaf of the firstfruits of your harvest to the priest."
(Leviticus 23:9-10 ESV)

The Lord wants us to come before Him with our harvest and thanksgiving to appreciate what He has done for us and blesses our lives. He is the One who teaches us to give so that what we gave will be measured back unto us shaken together, pressed down and be given back to us in full.

Give and it will be given to you: good measure, pressed down, shaken together, and running over will be put into your bosom. For with the same measure that you use, it will be measured back to you.
(Luke 6:38)

Bibliography

- Strong, James. S.T.D., L.L.D. 1890. <u>Strong's Exhaustive Concordance; Dictionaries of the Hebrew and Greek Words</u>. e-Sword ® version 7.6.1 Copyright © 2000-2005. All Rights Reserved. Registered trade mark of Rick Meyers. Equipping Ministries Foundation. USA www.e-sword.net.

- Unless otherwise indicated, all scriptural quotations are taken from the New King James Version®. Copyright © 1982 by Thomas Nelson, Inc. Used by permission. All rights reserved.

- Scripture references marked AKJV are taken from the American King James Version of the bible, a new English edition of the Holy Bible by Michael Peter (Stone) Engelbrite, based on the King James Version.

- Scripture references marked AMP are taken from The Amplified Bible. Old Testament copyright © 1965, 1987 by Zondervan Corporation, Grand Rapids, Michigan. New Testament copyright © 1958, 1987 by The Lockman Foundation, La Habra, California. All rights reserved.

- Scripture references marked ESV are taken from the ESV® Bible (The Holy Bible, English Standard Version®), copyright © 2001 by Crossway, a publishing ministry of Good News Publishers. Used by permission. All rights reserved.

- Scripture references marked KJV are taken from the King James Version of the bible.

- Scripture references marked NASB are taken from the New American Standard Bible®, Copyright © 1960, 1962, 1963, 1968, 1971, 1972, 1973, 1975, 1977, 1995 by The Lockman Foundation. Used by permission.

- Scripture references marked NIV are taken from The Holy Bible, New International Version® NIV®. Copyright © 1973, 1978, 1984, 2011 by Biblica, Inc.™ Used by permission of Zondervan Publishing House. All rights reserved worldwide.

- Scripture references marked NLT are taken from the Holy Bible, New Living Translation, copyright © 1996, 2004, 2007 by Tyndale House Foundation. Used by permission of Tyndale House Publishers, Inc., Carol Stream, Illinois 60188. All rights reserved.

- Scripture references marked NRSV are taken from the New Revised Standard Version Bible, copyright © 1989 the Division of Christian Education of the National Council of the Churches of Christ in the United States of America. Used by permission. All rights reserved.

❖
Ministry Profile
Apostle Dr Benjamin Ayim Asare

Dr. Benjamin Ayim Asare is an anointed minister of God with a strong deliverance flow, which is evident in all facets of his ministry. He is the president of **World Missions Ministries (WMM)** and the Senior Pastor of the **Followers of Christ International Church (FOCIC)** Novara, Italy.

Apostle Benjamin is the coordinator and the vice president of the Followers of Christ International Church. A member of **"Chiese Elim in Italia"** and holds Italian Ministerial Licenses "Ministro di culto." He also on the board of Lifestyle International Christian University (LICU) as an Executive Director, faculty member and is responsible for National Growth. On May 7th, 2013 Dr. Alan Pateman appointed Dr. Ayim Asare as an Executive Board Member of the International Apostolic accreditation council /IAAC) where he is responsible for the Association of Professionals.

Dr. Benjamin is a conference speaker, church planter, leadership mentor. He is an itinerant minister who ministers to organizations as well as groups and churches and ministers throughout nations.

In May 2010 Apostle Ayim Asare established the **"School of Ministry for Potential Leaders" (SOMFPL)** the aim is to provide training/seminar programs for ordinary people to potential leaders for the work of ministry, and that is to help them to identify their calling and ministry. This is the purpose and burden of the pastor and his leaders.

Dr. Benjamin is the owner of **"BENCOM Publication,"** publishing and distribution materials such as "Salvation is Free" for churches as Sunday school tools in English and in Italian and has authored several books.

This anointed man of God encourages thousands to answer the call of God through the teaching of the Word and dynamic demonstration of the Holy Spirit. His unique ability to identify the God-given gifting, calling and anointing upon God's people, through his proven dynamic teachings, draws the hearts of the people to our Lord and Saviour Jesus Christ as God's purpose is activated in their lives. Clearly, minds are renewed, lives are transformed and hearts are drawn to our heavenly Father as God's power and authority is magnificently displayed.

Apostle Dr. Benjamin Ayim Asare lives in Novara, Italy with his family.

www.benjaminayimasareministries.com
bayimasare@yahoo.it
focicatmissions@yahoo.com

To Contact the Author

Please email:

Followers of Christ International Church
c/o Apostle Benjamin Ayim Asare
Via Ghiberti, 1
Novara 28100
ITALY

Email: bayimasare@yahoo.it or
focicatmissions@yahoo.com

*Please include your prayer requests
and comments when you write.*

Other Books

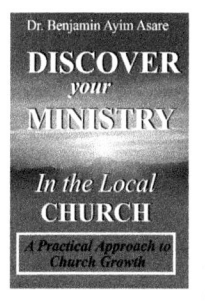

Discover your Ministry in the Local Church

When you begin to develop the ability to sever all alternatives and give total concentration and focus to the things that interests you most, you will discover incredible and remarkable success. Dr. Benjamin Ayim has provided a tool which will open your understanding to discover the purpose, the need and the practical approach of the ministry of helps in the local church.

ISBN: 978-0-9575775-1-0, Pages: 153,
Format: Paperback, Published: 2016

The Anointing is in the Assignment

The purpose of the anointing is for you as a Christian to live a victorious life and to witness the gospel message of Jesus Christ effectively. God wants to take ordinary people and work supernaturally through them to bring about a mighty move of His power, just the way He worked through His Son, Jesus Christ.

ISBN: 978-1-909132-07-8, Pages: 220,
Format: Paperback, Published: 2015

The Hand of the Diligent Will Rule

God has given us His resources of Time and Talent to receive money. You must remember that work is important to God. God values the work you do, because your work or job is equal to your time, talent and gifting. These gifts are God's resources and therefore God will not be happy with any of His children who take work for granted. Your work requires diligence, and excellent attitude determines good quality productivity.

ISBN: 978-0-957577-50-3, Pages: 120,
Format: Paperback, Published: 2013

Life is a Priceless Treasure

As you look beyond your time on earth, which in comparison with eternity, is just a brief moment, you will be assured that heaven, is your home. Time spent on earth is short. Yet this short time is very essential because it prepares you to receive everything needed in heaven.

BENCOM Publications, Pages: 47,
Format: Paperback, Published: 2008

From Deliverance to Inheritance

In this revolutionary book on deliverance, you will discover, understand and know the enemy, and know how you can take your strength in the Lord to overcome him in order to possess your inheritance.

BENCOM Publications, Pages: 129,
Format: Paperback, Published: 2008

- Italian Books -

La Vita è un Tesoro Inestimabile

Quando guardi al di là del tuo tempo sulla terra, che in confronto all' eternità è solo un breve momento, sarai sicuro che il cielo sarà la tua casa. Il tempo vissuto sulla terra è breve. Tuttavia, questi breve periodo di tempo è una cosa molto indispensabile, perchè ti prepara a ricevere tuute le cose di cui hai bisogno nel cielo.

ISBN 978-88-87511-90-1, Pages: 44,
Format: Paperback, Published: 2009

Dalla Liberazione all'Eredità

Libertà significa semplicemente uscire da una prigione o da problemi di legami economici, sociali e politici. Gesù fu mandato intenzionalmente da Dio per liberarci dal dominio del nemico.

ISBN 978-88-87511-85-7, Pages: 96,
Format: Paperback, Published: 2009

All Books Available

at

BENCOM PUBLICATIONS

Email: bayimasare@yahoo.it or
focicatmissions@yahoo.com

*Also Available from Amazon.com
and other retail outlets.*

www.ingramcontent.com/pod-product-compliance
Lightning Source LLC
Chambersburg PA
CBHW071624040426
42452CB00009B/1480